You May Relate

Reetu Chatterjee

INDIA · SINGAPORE · MALAYSIA

Index

Vida

Enjoy the current moment with joy & calm
    Life is very short,

Never focus on what you don't possess
We often don't receive what we thought.

Stop worrying about your future a lot,
Each scar, problem and situation heal with time, worry
you not!

Keep going and look for a bright future, you will be fine.

All you need to do is, heal yourself, value your life

And That is how

You will shine.

A Vital Acceptance

So much greed, so much pride for what?
Each one of us will perish one day
Believe it or not!

Today we are on earth,
Tomorrow we might become air.

From body to mud to ash
Apparently, life isn't too fair!

While you are alive enjoy each moment with presence
of mind

Joy is right in front of you, better chase it

"Hurry"

Don't be Blind

Learn to appreciate each moment as much as you could,

Life is not what others do
It's about
Do what you should.

A question to self

The urge to receive something is greater when we don't possess it,

However, it quickly gets shifted to something else when we receive it.

So how could you convince your mind and lie to your soul that you will be at bliss when you win something you currently lack?

Desires of the Dead

I am loaded, I earned a lot of money
But,
I couldn't earn time
Time for my family, kids, time for my honey.

I Travelled a lot but today I am stuck in the same place forever.

How funny it is, I have multiple accommodations, but none are really mine at this point of time

All I miss is the people I ignored, who craved my love, who cared for me!
But my greed pulled me back,

Oh lord put me back to life again

Prayed the man in the grave.

Para ti mi Amor

When I first saw you
You meant a Stranger to me

I Never imagined if both of us
Could ever make a "We"

All those months back as I can see
It all happened just the way it was meant to be

I am so grateful to have you by my side
This is dedicated to one, who is *MY GREATEST PRIDE*

Unsaid words of
the Secret Lover

I love your smile
I love your laughs
Your voice is soothing,
I love the way you talk.

I love your presence,
I crave your touch.
I love you way too much!

I love your hairs, I love your eyes
But more than everything, I love your soul

I want to attach with *what lies Inside.*

Absent Companion

I Speak to you even though I know
You do not exist.

I feel you even when I know
You are no reality,

For me, you are the healing
    I can't resist..

Together let's spend the life
With No one knowing my mind.

Painful Curiosity

I know you love her endlessly
But!
Why couldn't it to be me?

You stay with her Willingly,
Why couldn't it to be me?

You fear losing her desperately.
Why couldn't it to be me?

You crave her mentally.
Why couldn't it to be me?

After all
I was the one who stayed back when there was not
her, but every time,

It was *me!*

To my Dearest Un-existing Soul

I know you won't break my heart

I can feel you can't bear tears rolling down my cheeks,

I am aware that you genuinely care!

No other women excite you except for me

Nor will you let me feel insecure.

You love proving, only mine, you are!

You are the one I can count, without fear

After all reality hurts

Imagination doesn't.

An Angel blessed
by the Devil

Her eyes reflected the pain of her soul,

She had the power to make every word sound melodious.

Skin, as white as pearl.

Her lips were like the red rose petals on the white snow.

Her hairs were as shiny as satin,

Innocence reflecting through her Expressions while she spoke,

Yet, she was so evil deep down inside hiding a side no one imagined existed.

My dear Salvatore

She is me
I am her

We could never be Separated
We never were

She is my Shadow
I am her Support

She is kind
I am not

She is the pillar
I am the strength

She is what
I was once

A final Goodbye by the graveyard.

I still recall the day I begged you
Not to go,
You still left.

I never saw you again,

No one else did.

I waited!

While I knew you won't come

You never were there
Nor will you be.

It was all me every time

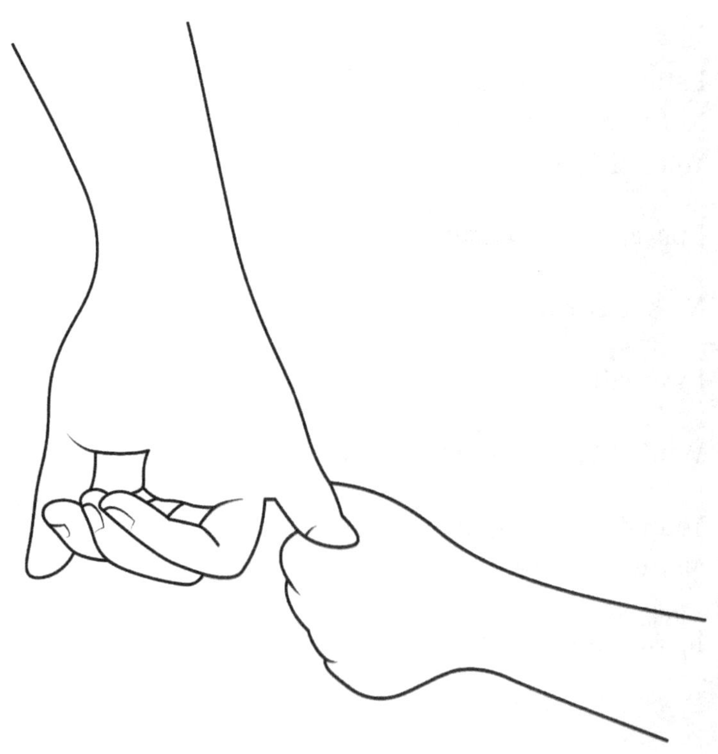

Someday, I must let you go

You are the bird, I don't want to Capture in a cage,

You are meant to fly!

But! What if I don't survive without you?

OH, Honey!

What If you conquer the sky?

Ma Cherie

Your hug is my home,
You are where I feel safe.

Your kiss quenches my thirst
You are the food which I crave.

Your touch is needed
Your affection is a must

You are all I have
Ma Cherie, I love you so much!

In less than no time

In less than no time, I started to love you

In less than no time, I trusted you

In less than no time, I imagined my future with you

In less than no time, I got afraid to lose you
How ever, you proved,
I should have taken more time

Promise under the moonlight

Let's grow old together,

Let's remove the clothes of lies and expose the skin of truth

Let's touch each other's soul with the hands that has never been touched

Let's kiss with the lips promising loyalty

Let's the eyes talk, which could only be heard in silence

Let's get laid together in the bed of commitment
Let's get intimate so deep that we could never come out of it due to its debt.

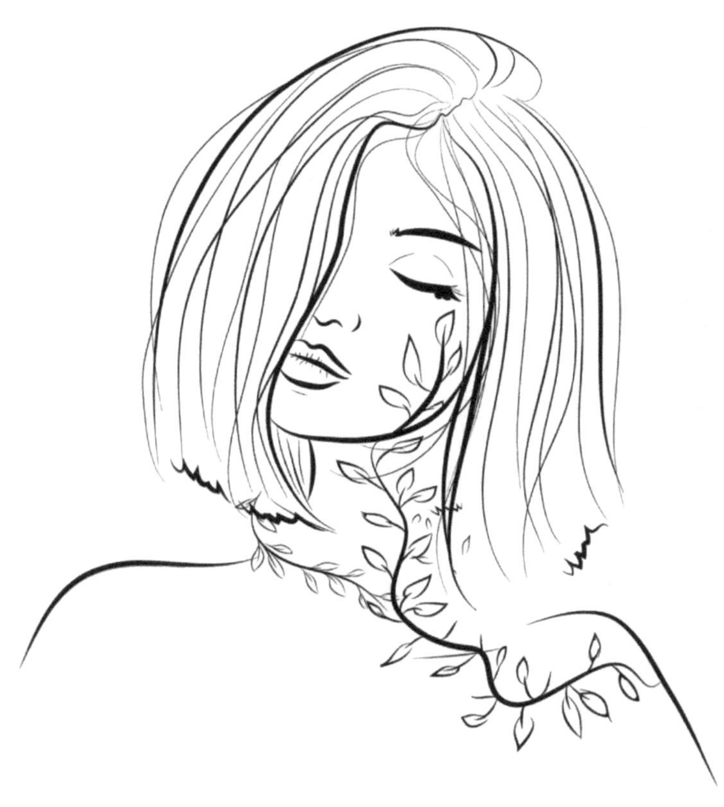

Midnight Thoughts!

How could I?
Lie to him, knowing that he could sense the pain behind these fake smiles.

How could I?
Lie to him, when I am aware he could hear the voice inside me screaming to be free from the prison of society.

How could I?
Lie to him, when he could sense the truth behind my lies.

How could I not tell him what he already knows and feels.

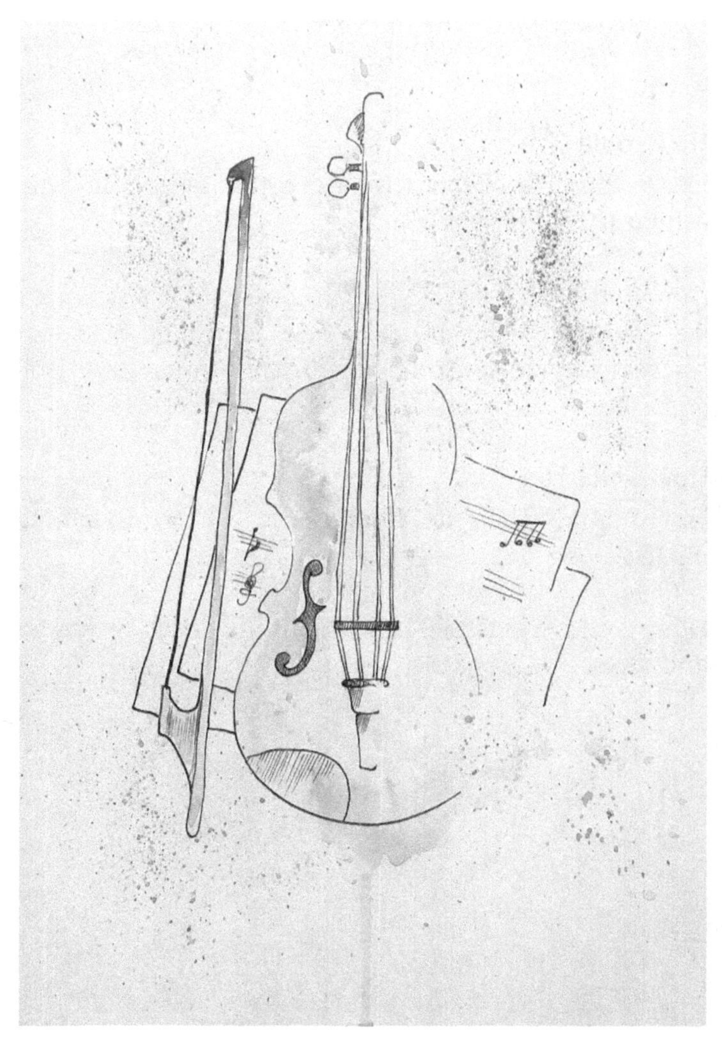

Destructive Attachment

They say you are supernatural but there i was
standing in the middle of the dark
With a blown-out candle, waiting for you to come
and light it,

Come, oh darling,
I crave for your dead soul,

Haunt me! I don't care

I need your presence
Let me feel your breath

I am in the middle of the forest
Where are you, my love?

Him Or Nothing

Why him? They Asked?

Because he made me feel the way each soul desires to be felt.
He had an insight of my insecurity and had the urge to make sure I never felt this way.

He stayed, when everybody left,
He loved me the way I was.

He had an acceptance of fact that I was imperfect and always focused on the perfections that lied with me.
Unlike others he was never afraid to touch me, when I had unhealed wounds all over

So rather ask me
Why not him?

An underrated way
of loving

You know you love a bird when you don't cage her but set her free.

Similarly,

you know you love a person when you don't tie them to the chain of your limitations but set them free with,

loyalty, care, security and commitment...